THINGS I NEEDED

THINGS I NEEDED

Taylor Little

Burlington,
Vermont

Onion River Press
Burlington, VT 05401
info@onionriverpress.com
www.onionriverpress.com

ISBN: 978-1-957184-68-5
Library of Congress Control Number: 2024912419

INTRODUCTION

Part memories, part imagination, part novel, part play, part sudden thoughts—that's what makes up this collection. I never dreamed of sharing it this way, but I'm here for it...and here you are. Amazing!

Everything shared here is a reflection or realization that I've experienced from what I call an Eyes Closed Practice. Basically, listening to music with my eyes closed, often combined with a form of movement and breathwork. The songs I've used in my Eyes Closed Practices are too many to count (plus that one I listened to over 3,000 times in one year), so I'll take a moment here to thank everyone involved in creating all the songs I've listened to on repeat. To the singers, musicians, composers, songwriters, sound engineers, producers—everyone. Thank you forever.

The title is *Things I Needed* because I used to be convinced that I didn't "need" anything. It took me a long time to believe that not only was it okay to need some things, but that I could actually change my life if I embraced needing and (if I was *really* honest) wanting to be close to people, close to experiences, and to feel all that life can feel.

I won't say it's been easy—the main things I needed to start were time, space, and patience. But once I was able to give myself those things often enough, everything else started becoming clear. And another thank you forever to the once-in-a-lifetime coach who can hold fires and rivers and who offered me all the time, space, and patience I needed before I could offer any to myself. I would not have found a way on my own.

All of this has come together spontaneously. In a way that I fell into spontaneously. I guess that's how it had to happen. I never could have planned it. Everything here was written in a four-year span, beginning and ending on a February 29; a beautiful time-bending day. The month is added to each entry to give some sense of the moment in time. The order shared is not chronological, but it's what feels correct. My hope is that you can flip to any page on any day. Maybe you'll happen upon something you needed too.

The last thing I'll offer to you here is this: Don't think too much about it.

For You.

Let it overflow this universe. And I'll know it's you in the next one.

CONTENTS

THINGS I NEEDED TO FEEL

I Know How It Feels

I know how it feels to not be loved so much
It feels like I never existed.

And I know how it feels to be loved so much
It feels like I'm all that ever existed.

I'm Loving You

I remember when you first said it to me
"I'm loving you"
I'd never heard it like that before
It felt so active
Like *right in this second*
I'm loving you
It was so present, or it felt that way to me
And presence was always a shock
You said it in a quiet moment
I'm loving you
As though there was nothing else in the world to do

The next time you said it wasn't a quiet moment
At the time, I wished that moment hadn't happened

I hated that moment
And yet, I can still remember you saying
I'm loving you
As the floor fell out, the roof flew off, and the
walls gave way
I remember hearing
I'm loving you

Now one of my favorite moments
Even more than the quiet one in a way
Just in the worst
With the worst
I'm loving you

How many moments you did that for me
How many moments when you said
I'm loving you
And the moment I finally could for you

When I said, “You don’t have to come with me” as
I picked up the keys
And you didn’t answer, just kept tying your shoe
Before you stood up, I saw you wipe away a tear
And I just thought
I’m loving you
I turned and looked out the window
One of so many moments when I didn’t know
what to do
I didn’t know if you wanted it acknowledged

But I’m loving you

I turned back around, you were putting on your
coat
I took the two steps over to you and touched
your hand gently
You wrapped mine up
Gripping it

It felt like you didn't want to let go
I'm loving you

I saw another tear
You closed your eyes and put your other hand
over your face
My hand still wrapped in yours, I sat down on the
bench where you'd been tying that shoe
You sat next to me, a sharp inhale as you did
I squeezed your hand when I felt it start to shake
And then whispered
"I'm loving you"

Nothing About Me Was Broken

One beautiful moment when I can honestly say I wasn't scared, I wasn't running, I wasn't in an altered state, I didn't believe it was wrong, I didn't think I had to hide, I didn't have to be silent, I didn't have to be anything I thought I did.

Before any of the healing things, before any of that, there was this moment.

A moment when I had my mind, my eyes, my voice, my body, my heart all together. All there, all along.

I needed the healing things to help me remember, though. How we wind back onto ourselves and see through clearer eyes.

Because nothing about me was broken.

But in one beautiful moment, everything I thought about everything about me is shattered.

Nowhere Else To Be

I could see my legs shaking, my hands shaking.

I hated when they shook; I felt like I was so exposed. Anyone could see.

I had to make it stop. The harder I tried to make it stop, the more everything shook.

Then you came over and sat down beside me. Slowly, like you were gliding.

You didn't say anything, didn't try to touch me or move anything. Just sat down.

I looked away, but I could feel you looking straight ahead. Not glaring at me. Just a soft gaze, a soft breath next to me. Nowhere else to be except here with me.

I felt almost ashamed that you were sitting with me. I wanted to believe that you wanted to be somewhere else, that you were bored or frustrated.

But I could feel you weren't.

I don't know why, but you weren't.

You Breathe More Easily Up There

I knew it was you as soon as I saw that picture.
Hidden in there.
Brow furrowed.
She knew you were there too.
Knew that you were looking out at us.
Watching.
Watching the horizon, watching the ground.
Always there even if we didn't always see you.
But that isn't all of you.
You can fly too.
Gliding through the air with nothing holding you down.
I can feel you breathe more easily up there.
And as the ashes fall, I feel you getting lighter,
flying so smoothly over the waves.
Let's stay by the water forever.

July

Armor

This is what a sternum looks like.
Have you ever broken one?
It hurts.
It's covered in armor now.
I don't even know what the bone looks like
anymore.
But when I hold the song to my chest, the armor
vibrates.
Maybe I can get it off.

Sweet Songs

Sometimes I put on really pop-y love songs. The over-the-top sweetness is what I need on certain days. The intense unrealisticness of it. I can see so many scenes going with those songs. Scenes from my life, and scenes I imagine. Beautiful moments that are captured perfectly by the melody.

Most of the songs are upbeat, with a big crescendo moment when the "love" just bursts through the speakers. Well, maybe it isn't love. It's that sweetness again, it spills over. A lot of the time, sweetness makes me sick. I'd always choose a salty snack. But some days, I crave this sweet. The half-smiles people in the videos for these songs always exchange. The unbound exuberance. Ecstatic energy. It's probably why the songs are catchy.

I started putting on sweet songs about a week ago. The first one is really sweet. Eesh. And then another last night. Yikes. I want to cringe at it, but I feel joy. And now a third today. Surely it's one of the top sweet pop songs of the last decade. I heard it in the grocery store. They're all songs that could make me roll my eyes on other days, but these past few days they've all just made me half-smile. I won't lie, it feels good to let the unrealistic, exuberant, ecstatic sweetness in sometimes.

A Scab

"I wanted to tell you a million times."

"Why didn't you?"

I laugh almost.

"It wasn't like we were talking. I hadn't heard from you in over a year. It never seemed like you wanted to hear from me." I pause. "I don't know actually, it kinda did seem like you wanted to hear from me, but then you would just stop responding."

"I'm sorry."

"I'm not mad about it. And I wasn't then. I never have been. I don't know how to say that without you hearing it like it's not true. But it's true."

"I just didn't have space."

"I know. That's why I stopped. But I was also afraid you would think I didn't care about you. Or that I was mad. But I did care, and I wasn't mad. I wanted you to know that. And every time I thought about reaching out to you again, I had to walk myself back from those things. Because I had told you I cared about you. And I meant it when I said I wasn't mad."

"Honestly, I can't believe you're still thinking about it."

"Me either." Sharpening.

"I don't know what to say."

"Me either." Softening.

"I don't know what will change."

"Me either."

I don't know why I keep having this conversation with you. Going over again and again what we say and what will happen after. How it will feel. When all along I know. Sometimes I think it's a gift to myself. But other times it's picking at a scab. Healed and opened so many times. This time it's a scab. It's bleeding right now. I think I was just bored.

I Love You, I Love You, I Love You

I don't mean for this to be in any way depressing or morbid, but I want to share something beautiful that also includes someone passing on. Someone I love so much. I love them incomprehensibly. I don't have a lot of experience with feelings like this, so I still find it hard to know what words to use.

What I do know is I could not have written it as beautifully as it happened. We knew things were coming to an end, so it wasn't unexpected, but it happened quickly. So quickly. I put on music, and ended up stopping the mix at one particular song. I kept it on repeat. They rested their palm on my cheek, and I put my hand over theirs. We listened to that song so many times. "It's so peaceful," they said with their eyes closed. We were just there in it. I was crying all kinds of tears. They kept their palm right on my cheek, and I leaned into it. Their last words to me were, "I love you, I love you, I love you." And I saw them go.

It's devastating to lose those we love. To lose them in the form we've always known them. And it's devastating to leave those we love. To know they can't come with us as we go. Devastating all around. Unbearable sometimes. There is absolutely no denying that.

But of all the infinite ways to feel devastated in the losing and the leaving, here we got to experience this beautiful version in both, which I never imagined could also exist.

One Second

Love me for one second.

It was more a hope in that moment than anything I'd ever say to anyone.

I needed to get out.

So I took a blanket from the end of the bed and went into the other room, finding a spot on the floor in the dark and pulling the blanket over me.

I heard you stir a few minutes later. I kept my eyes closed. It would be easier in the morning.

You moved around the bed, gathering up all the blankets, and then I felt you covering me with them.

I felt the warmth before I realized what it was.

You didn't say anything or even touch me; you just lay down on the floor, too, a few inches away.

And then I heard you sleeping.

One second.

The Best Of Them

So many things they did around me were out of
pain, guilt, or fear.
But the things they did for me were out of love.

So it wasn't that they didn't love me or didn't love
me as much.
What they did for me, that was their love.

Small spots of light.

To be one of the few who got love.
Not pain, guilt, or fear.

So even if I still don't know about the phrase "the
best they could,"
I know I got the best of them.

This Isn't A Fight

"Hi Love," you said. You're the only one who calls me that.

I stood in the doorway. The room was mostly dark, just one lamp on a side table glowing warmly. I was glad the overhead lights were off. The sky was a soft gray through the windows, navy blue clouds filling in as the last bit of sunlight faded.

You were lying in bed, where you'd been for awhile. Your eyes were closed; I don't know how you knew it was me at the door.

I walked over to the side of the bed. You didn't open your eyes, just moved over a few inches. I lay down next to you, and you pulled the blanket over us and put your arms around me.

“Hi Love,” you said again. My body had never felt softer than right then.

I felt the tears rising and almost tried to stop them before letting them go. You rested your thumb between my eyebrows, gently smoothing where the furrow formed. “This isn’t a fight,” you said. “You don’t have to fight this.” After a moment you added, “Neither of us have to fight this.” Your voice was quiet, you’d aged so much. As more love came in, more fight went out.

You breathed deeply. “Of anyone in this world, I’m so glad to have been proved wrong by you,” you said and squeezed me. I closed my eyes and tried to submerge myself in that moment. Tried to let it soak in, to the bone. But I felt myself scrunching up, sinking. “Come on now,” you said, feeling it too, “that’s not you.” I opened my eyes and you brought your thumb back between my eyebrows. “Let this be beautiful,” you said softly.

Sore From Smiling

I laughed really hard today.

We sang together and did all the voices.

It was fun, so I just brought it back up.

And it's amazing how easy it was to sing along and have facial expressions.

I remembered I've done that before.

I've been on a stage before.

I've had to make up something in front of an audience before, and it was easy and fun.

And then for so long I didn't and wasn't and it was hard.

I can feel my face knows though.

I remember being sore from smiling.

Hearing her laughing so hard, and I'm laughing at how hard she's laughing.

I remember that feeling.

October

Your Palm

I feel your hand on my back. I love that. Just a palm, right in the middle, right where it used to hurt. Feels like I can breathe into it. I want to turn around but then I think I shouldn't. That Orpheus myth stuck.

But my favorite interpretation is actually one I heard not that long ago: That Eurydice made a sound on purpose so Orpheus would turn around. I love that too—her decision. Changes the whole story. And maybe not a popular interpretation because it kinda cuts out the romantic part. Well, in a way. I stopped in my tracks when I heard it though. A story so well known and given that was suddenly completely different.

I can still feel your palm, resting gently, right in the middle. I take a breath and look over my shoulder. I knew you'd be there.

This Silence

Can I call you? I finally typed in.
We usually only texted.
I felt the urgency though.
...You typing...
And then I saw the words *Of course.*
So I called. No video.
"Hi," you said. I could hear your smile.
But I couldn't say anything.
"Hi," you said again, your voice going quieter.
I held the phone in front of me. Looking at your name on the screen.
"I don't know," I finally got out.
"I know," you said.

Then a silence filled everything.

I've been in lots of different silences. Silences don't bother me. I was used to hollow silence. Empty silence. Cold silence. Awkward silence, sure. But this silence was comforter soft. Pillowy and warm. Wrapping up us and the space and everything. I could hear you were there, even though I couldn't hear any noise. This silence was full. And we lay in it for a long time. I pulled it closer.

I wanted to tell you. But instead we stayed there in that silence. Until I fell asleep. When I woke up, it was still dark. I didn't know what time it was. I felt around for the phone, but the screen was blank. I made my way to the other room and found the charger, plugged in the phone, and lay back down. When the screen lit up again, four words from you. Even in silence, you know what I need to hear.

You Were Gentle Instead

I was thinking about you this morning.
You just popped into my head.
I never thanked you—for not destroying me.
I never thanked you for that, so I will, even just here.

Thank you.

You could have destroyed me, and you didn't.
And you knew you could have, but you didn't.
You were gentle instead.
You were always so gentle instead.

All I See Is You

There are infinite places and living things in this world,
And all I see is you.

There are infinite worlds in space,
And all I see is you.

You see this world and you see the other worlds,
And all I see is you.

The Most Loved

The moment I felt the most loved
It wasn't that long ago
I felt the most loved and the most love
The softest and deepest
I startled away
Arms gently reached out
Come back to me
And I did
Fear watched from the side
Even it felt the soft and the deep
Even it could see that love exists too
Here in the cells
Just like it does
It isn't alone after all

This Was A Never

Never forget this moment
How you feel right now
How you're crying and laughing and smiling
And feeling everything at the same time

Never forget this moment
I'm so glad you're getting to have this moment
You used to try to say things like, "Never say never"
But maybe didn't really believe it because *this* was a "never"

But it's not
It's here right now

No One Else Could Ever Love Me Like This

A firelit room in a stone house.
A bed with big pillows and a big blanket.
It's so warm.
The window is open, one broken shutter
creaking.
The sky is purple, slow waves rolling in.
And then I see her hand on the window ledge,
and you in her hand.
And you giving her a boost from outside.
She climbs in, and you lower her down from the
window.
She helps you over to me, and you rest your
cheek on mine.
No one else could ever love me like this.

Grand-Titi

If I'm a mommy and have kids, will they have a Titi?

Maybe. Maybe I can be their Titi too.

Yes. You'll be the Grand-Titi.

Soft

I caught you in my arms softly
You're not weak
You're not fragile
You are indestructible
I don't think kid gloves ever even fit
It's not soft because it's pity
It's not soft because it's scared
Let your eyes see
Let that space where your ribs meet feel
It's just soft because it's soft
Look at me softly
The way they looked at you
It's right here
Let it be beautiful
Because it already is

Love Me More

And when you love me so much it hurts
Love me more
And when the sun rises in the west
Love me more
And when the anchors fall away
Love me more
And when you're trying so hard
Love me more
And when oblivion appears
Love me more
And when you think you can't
Just love me more

The pain isn't me.
The fear isn't me.
The past isn't me.

The future isn't me.

Love me.

Love me more than all of that.

Right now.

But It's For You

Just try sitting here with me
We don't have to go too far
And if you're not sure, take my hand
'Cause it's not like we're planting our
Feet standing on the ground
We're barely standing on the ground

If we were floating, maybe that'd feel fine
One's not better, don't have to define
What it's supposed to look like
Or where we should go
I'm just glad you're here beside me
That's all we need to know

I wonder how long you were standing
Out in the rain there all alone

Without your boots on, no coat, nothing
Soaking to the bone
So come in now by the fire
It's warm and soft with blankets here
Dry your hair, your feet, your eyes
There's nothing left to fear

And I'll sit with you forever more
For longer than you think is for

You

But it's for you

Space That Has Never Felt Breath

"Get out of my life," I said slowly but still loudly, glaring right at them.

I waited for the wobble, when something in me would want them to stay—but it didn't come.

As the days passed, still no wobble. All I felt was the space I let them take up. I felt it for the first time. How much space I let them take up. How I had been breathing around them. Into tiny cracks on the sides. It's hard to describe how it feels to breathe into a space that has never felt breath before.

I still expect them everywhere. In a way, I still want them there. Fear has a kind of comfort in its certainty. And my fear is certain about them.

Open space, though, this is still new.

Every Moment, Every Moment

It hurts.
It only hurts because there's a wall. Love me so much it opens.
I can't.
You can.
I'm scared.
What are you scared of?
I'll fall.
There's nowhere to fall. I'll hold you forever.
What's forever?
Every moment, every moment.
Nothing is forever.
This is. Do you believe me?
No.
That's okay. We'll keep coming here. One day you'll believe me.

Back And Forth

I'd never been in this room before
But I felt the pleading
And I didn't know where it was coming from
Please
In pain
Urgent
Please
A rocking chair appears
We'll just sit here
Back and forth
That's all we need

Never Have To Explain It To Me

They'll never understand, but I do.
Is that the shadow of something else, though?
No, it's just you.
Sounds like a bad thing.
Maybe not. You get to decide. No one else decides.
Maybe I just am.
Yeah, I know you are.
I don't want to have to explain it.
You never have to explain it to me.

The Only Place I Want To Be

I feel you there so clearly.
Making your way over to me.
Wrapping me up. Hugging me. Squeezing.
It's all so soft and gentle, and time becomes nothing.

That's you.

And I can feel how that's you.
How it's so natural for you.
I'm so aware of how natural it is for you.
It feels easy with you, but I know it wasn't easy for you.

And all I can say is, this is the only place I want to be.

The Most And Forever

I was feeling very alone in myself.
That personal betrayal was still really active.
Then she appeared, holding my hand.
I was facing one way; she was facing the other way.
We're each holding our left hands.
And she's holding you in her right hand.
She's holding my hand so tightly and leaning her head against my arm.
She brought me back in.

I turn, and all of them are there.
A sense that they're here for me too.
"I believe in you, I believe in this, I'm right here," she says.
And they all say the same thing.

And you see that everything you're protecting thinks we don't need to do it that way.

Then she says to you, "I love you the most and forever. You're my most favorite. *This* is you too. Remember that this is you too."

And you say, "I remember."

That Moment Led Me To This One

It didn't matter what you did.

It didn't matter how long it took.

In that moment it was real.

And that moment led me to this one.

It hurts.

And I'm also grateful to you for helping me see this.

A Voice I Love

It loves me so much.
It's saying everything I want to hear.
In a voice I love.
But two words give it away.
It's trying so hard, but it can't hide.
I almost didn't see it.
I almost didn't.
Then I did.
And I love it more now.

Farewell

I walked for hours today. Listening to the same song over and over. A song without words. It's not a new song, but I haven't heard it for a long time.

As I listened, I had a familiar feeling. I remember the feeling from when I first heard this song. From when I bought the CD with bonus tracks and still only listened to this one. Over and over, even then.

And as I'm listening now, I realize the number 19 appears again. My mind still can't explain that. All the nineteens. It really wants to explain them, but with this one it falls silent. How can it explain this? It can't. I can't, I guess.

I keep walking, and then my mind starts to urge: *Change to a new song*. But I don't want to change it. I want to hear it again and again and feel it again and again. I stop and close my eyes right in the middle of the path.

And suddenly as the music rises, I start dropping everything I'm holding, one by one letting them fall. Pulling off all the heaviness from shoulders, wrists, legs, chest, and I start running. And then a feeling of jumping out, gliding and weightless. I open my eyes, and I'm still standing in the middle of the path. I hear the birds singing the name. "Farewell," I say softly.

A Reminder

You know.

You knew.

You don't have to look for me.

I'm right here.

I'll always be right here.

THINGS I NEEDED TO HEAR

Infinite Universes

And in all the infinite universes

I choose you.

To Me Then From Me Now

You think you'll have to forgive everything. You
don't.
You think you'll have to tell every detail. You
don't.
You think you'll have to leave. You don't.
You think you'll have to cry the whole time. You
don't.

You think you'll never laugh. You will.
You think you'll never come out if you go in. You
will.
You think you'll never feel differently. You will.
You think you'll never believe it. You will.

You think no one could understand. Someone
could.

You think no one could care. Someone could.
You think no one could hold it. Someone could.
You think no one could stay. Someone could.

You think you can't do it. You can.

You think you don't matter. You do.

But I see now that you already knew all that.

So maybe this is actually a reminder to Me Now from Me Then.

This Is Yours

This is yours.

Let it be so bright you can't look away.

And let it be so beautiful you don't want to miss a second.

Pyrrhic

It's shaking in my jaw and chest first. Like I'm going to throw up. It's moving up my throat and I gag. My legs are shaking and pressing together. My arms are wrapped around my chest. I keep saying, "Okay, okay." Now my palms are pressing into my head. My eyes are blinking fast; tears pour, obscuring any view. I'm looking all around, but I can't see anything and I don't want to close my eyes. I lie on my side, press my forehead into the floor, and curl my knees in as close as I can. Everything is shaking. I can't see. And I can feel my hands pressing into my head, but I can't feel my head pressing into the floor. I roll onto my back and look at the ceiling but that's worse—my chest feels like it will break. I move against the couch and push into it. Maybe it will be stable since I'm not. I pull a blanket over my head and bring it down to my chest. "You don't have to do anything ever." That's new. I start repeating it to myself. Aloud. The voice is mine, but my body doesn't recognize it. I keep repeating, "You don't have to do anything ever." Over and over. The tears slow down. I find something to look at—my fingers against the blanket. They're not shaking now. I take the blanket off my head. I put my hands over my eyes but keep my eyes open. I sit there for awhile.

And then I decide I will write this since I actually remember it all. Also new.

It's as I read it that I hear: "You win. You've always won." A pause, and then a genuine, and new, question, "But is this worth it?"

I Just Love You

You looked me right in the eyes and said:

I don't love who they think you are.

I don't love who you think you are.

I just love you.

Beautiful Starlit Somewhere

The light was so bright.
Piercing through everything I thought I could see.
And then there she was.
I knew her right away but couldn't believe what I was seeing.
Right in front of me.
The stars glinting behind her through the frame, lighting up what looked like nothing before.
"Where have you been?" I asked, my voice shaking.
She smiled. "I've been here, waiting for you."
I looked down. I felt like I was reaching and running away, like I might split apart.
All the faces looking up at me.

"You watched me leave. You knew?" I said, trying to understand.

"I knew you'd come back." She glanced down at them.

"How long would you have waited?"

She almost shrugged. "Forever. But that time isn't anything. Every moment I loved you. You're my love."

I recoiled. It hurt to hear. "How can I be?"

She smiled again and tilted her head gently.

"You just are. And now, here in this beautiful starlit Somewhere, we watched you come back."

What You Think It Is

"What if it isn't what you think it is?"
A hundred different ways in a hundred different tones.
"What if it isn't what you think it is?"
"What if it isn't what you think it is?"
Over and over.
"No, it is, it definitely is."
I'm certain.
"What if it isn't what you think it is?"
I reposition everything.
The song, my body.
"It definitely is."
"But what if it isn't."
Until I finally turn off the music and stop moving.
And then, right there.
It isn't what I thought it was.

I'm Right Here

Back pressed against couch, knees pulled in,
arms wrapped around legs.
I'm right here, I'm right here.

Feeling what I've never felt.
I'm right here, I'm right here.

What needed to happen then, what feels like is
happening now.
I'm right here, I'm right here.

The tears are overflowing, but my eyes are still.
The breath is gasping, but I can feel it is deep.
The words are pained, but my voice is steady.
I'm right here, I'm right here.

I’m with me then. Now.
I can feel it then. Now.

This is hard.

I’m right here.

I Wanted To Hear Your Voice

I remember your last words to me were, "I
wanted to hear your voice."
No one had ever said that to me before.
I couldn't imagine someone wanting to hear my
voice actually.
There was a long time when no one did hear it,
when I didn't hear it.
I didn't even consider anyone would want to.
And even as all of this happened, I didn't think
my voice was part of it.

That's been a massive shift in my life, that my
voice is part of it.
You helped with that.
You probably didn't know that.

I still feel sad that those were the last words you said to me.
I feel sad at how beautiful those words are in so many ways, in that situation, in that moment.
I'm crying thinking about it right now.

Just Let Me Be Here

I can't do this.
You don't have to do anything.
But you want me to.
You don't have to do anything.
You don't understand.
You're right, in a lot of ways I don't.
You want me to feel differently.
I mean, I don't want you to be in pain.
You think it will all just go away.
No. I don't think that.
I wish you'd leave me alone.
I know.
Just let me be here.
Okay.

Stay Open

I lean against your back.

You roll over and wrap me up.

I want to stay here forever.

"You're here," you say, knowing.

I've heard it before, but this is a different way.

"I want to stay *here*, though," I insist.

"Don't close over, Beautiful, stay open."

You Don't Have To Be Anything

I loved you when you did good things.
I loved you when you did terrible things.

You don't have to be anything.

Just you.
Just this.

I Never Used To Cry

I started crying as soon as I saw it.
I felt so angry.
And I felt so hopeless because after everything I still started crying almost immediately.
I then felt angry at how much I was crying.
I never used to cry.

I was on the floor in the bathroom.
"Do you still love me?" I asked.
"Of course," you said.
"Even with everything?"
"You are everything."

I'll Come Right Back

And I'm crying
And I'm saying "please come back"
And then, in the image, they turn around and say
"I'll come right back"
That's what I needed to hear

Their hands on my cheeks
Their face right in front of me
And I'm sobbing and it's okay
"I'll come right back"
I knew it couldn't happen then, but it can happen now

"I'll come right back, I'll come right back"
I say it over and over and over

You're Doing It

I wonder where you'll be when you read this again. I wonder what moment will bring you back to it. I hope a joyful one. But if it isn't, that's okay, and I hope it helps remind you that this is not hopeless. It never was.

Staying with yourself is the most incredible thing of your life. If you're with you, look at what can happen. You can feel and be with so much. Deep and true with yourself is a different world. You're doing it.

Nothing specific, no timeline. Every day, you just keep listening, and here we are. Wherever we are.

And in case you need to hear one of these in this moment:

"Things aren't the same,"

"I'm right here," and

"Nobody loves you like I do."

Not Someone Else. You.

These tears are so full.
Saturated, heavy.
These aren't scared tears.
These are old tears.

Weighted with years.
Weighted with depth.
But not gone.
Even though we tried.

These are the tears that never came out because we were never here.
These tears needed someone here.

Not someone else. You.

It's Okay To Stop

You're trying really hard.
I know you're trying.

And I know you don't like when people say you don't have to try, or that you never had to try, or that for you things just happen without trying.

None of those are true.
But you don't have to try all the time with this.
There's nowhere to get to.
Not not-caring.
But not pushing something before it feels ready.

It's okay to stop.

Do you feel like it's okay to stop?

Are you scared it will all go back?

I know you're scared you'll feel how you used to feel.

But you don't have to go back there if you don't choose to.

You do have a choice.

And it's okay to make a different one.

And it's okay if the choice is to stop.

Stopping isn't going back, it's just a pause.

This Is A Lot

I know this is a lot.

See if you can let it fill you up,

Not shut you down.

June

Behind A Closed Door

I saw the door right in front of me, and I knew she was on the other side. I could hear her screaming, smashing things, and punching against it.

I went up to the door and sat down.

"Hey, where are you?" I said. "Where did you go?"

The other side quieted. I felt her pressing against the door; she definitely didn't want to open it.

"I'm just sitting here," I offered. "I'm not going to come in. Will you talk to me here?"

I heard her take a breath on the other side.

"I thought it would be different," she finally said.

"Which part?" I asked gently.

"I thought they would care." Her voice was sharp, harsh.

I took a breath. “You don’t know that they don’t,” I said softly. “There’s so much meaning in that.”

I could hear her start to crumble. And then a swooshing sound as she slid down to the ground, still leaning against the door to make sure no one came in.

“I feel like I really believed it, though.” Her voice broke, and I could hear the tears falling.

A softening, an opening even behind a closed door.

“That doesn’t mean it wasn’t true,” I said as I heard her tears getting louder. I could feel her pain coming right through the door.

“It’s not that it wasn’t true then. It’s not that it wasn’t true then,” I repeated. “And it’s not that it wasn’t real. And I know you wish it would stay, but you’re the only one who can stay. You’re the only one who can stay. Don't go chasing after them."

"Why does it always feel like this happens?" The hopelessness had seeped into her voice. I knew what she was thinking.

"I think somewhere you're expecting it always." I decided to just be honest. "I think you know. You believe it will happen. And then it feels like that's what happens because that's the meaning that you're putting on those actions, right?"

"But I'm not making it up," she snapped.

"No, it's not made up, you're not wrong. But that's not everything. It's not the only way."

"I hate how this feels."

I could feel her wanting to barricade herself in there.

"I know. I know. But you can't change them."

She was curling in on herself, but there was still a softness, an openness to being here with me.

We sat for a bit.

"You're gripping so tightly to those moments," I continued. "They're weighing a thousand pounds. We can't change what they do, right? I know you really wish it were different. I know it's really hard to believe that it still matters, but it does. You know you get there. I know you get there. I know you'll get there. I know you will."

Screaming

You're not screaming in an empty room.

You're right here with me.

Knot

I had a knot in my chest this past week.
It was tight, and I could feel how strong and thick it was.
I didn't know how to loosen it, let alone untie it.

I don't remember exactly how it started to come undone.

Maybe it was the kind way he said, "Hey, what's going on?" when I called from the middle of an anger and frustration whirlpool.

Or the way she leaned into me while we sat on the couch.

I don't know.

I like to think they helped, though.

But I think it was really when I heard, "Voilà, voilà, voilà"—like, okay, here it is, this is what we're working with.

Voilà, voilà, voilà.

That Looks Heavy

"I don't have to do anything ever," I said defiantly, throwing one of the most beautiful things you ever said, and the most powerful thing I ever heard, right back in your face.
And I threw it at you hard.
I want to say I don't know why I do that, but I do know.
Your eyes clear, you just smiled, raising an eyebrow.
You know, too.

"No. You don't." Your voice still soft, unsurprised and unfazed.
"Well, I don't," I said.
But I felt the stone and metal grating together.
I felt the reverberation in my teeth.

“Of course you don’t,” you said.

I looked down.
We stood in silence for awhile.
I wasn’t thinking anything.
Nothing.
I didn’t want you to hear even a thought.

After some time you said, “Of course you don’t have to do anything. But if you want to, I’m here.”
You paused. “And that looks heavy.”
I kept looking down. But I knew it was heavy. And I felt tired.
“It’s not that easy,” I said.
“It’s not hard either,” you countered.

You. Right Here.

You don't have to redeem anything.
You're trying to stop someone from doing something.
You're screaming, *Stop, wake up!*
Listen.
You.
Right here.
Stop.
Stop.
You can't stop their story.
But you can stop running after them, thinking it will change yours.

And Then He Says

It's funny how the same words said in a certain tone or with a certain energy can feel so completely different. And it's the same with an action.

We're driving, and he's going to drop me off. And he asks, "Have you ever done this before?" And I say, "No." And he nods and offers some suggestions.

Then he says, "Do you have your phone?" And I say, "No," because there's no signal so I didn't bring it. And he looks concerned.

After a second he says, "I don't love that you don't have a phone." He looks out over the steering wheel. Really thoughtfully.

We get to the spot.

As I'm leaving, he says, "Okay, remember what I said before."

And then he says:

"If you're not back by four o'clock, I'm going to come find you. So if something happens, just stay where you are—I'll find you."

And for some reason, that feels really comforting. *I'll find you.* And those same words could feel so threatening. I believe how he's saying it, though.

That he'll find me because he actually cares if I'm okay. And we just met 10 minutes ago.

And then, like he knows what I'm thinking, he says again, sincerely, "If something happens, don't worry, I'll find you, we'll get you home."

April

Infinite Piece Puzzle

You seemed distracted. Then I saw you kneeling on the floor, spreading something out in front of you. I walked over.

"What are you working on?"

"My puzzle," you said, without looking up.

"It's big. So many beautiful scenes made up of such small pieces."

"Yeah," you said quickly, still not looking at me.

"It seems like you're rushing."

"I want all the pieces to fit together."

I looked at the box of puzzle pieces next to you. You were holding that box so tightly to your chest yesterday. Now I know why.

"Yeah, I know you want that," I said.

That's when you stopped and looked at me,
"Don't take any."
"I won't."

The box was overflowing.

You paused and then said quietly, "I tried to start with the edge pieces but couldn't find them all. But I know that's how you're supposed to do a puzzle."
I tilted my head to look at what you'd done so far. "I think this is an infinite piece puzzle, so maybe there are no edges really."
"Mm," you sighed. "Well, I can put together these pieces really fast now." Your voice lightened there.
"Yeah, I love the images those pieces make. That box is full, though, isn't it, always?"

You looked at it. "I guess so. But I need all the pieces."

"No one can take them away from you. Is it okay if it's an infinite piece puzzle? Are you going to carry that box with you forever?"

"Maybe," you said, your voice sliding sharply.

I nodded. "You can. You can also leave it here if you want and come work on it when you feel like it. You don't have to pack it up and then start again every time."

You furrowed your brow. "What if something messes it up?"

"Nothing can mess it up here. None of it can be taken from you. If you want, you can leave it as you have it here and come add pieces when you find them. But you don't have to carry it if you don't want to."

Two Sentences

1. You are not the reason for their pain.

2. You didn't disappear, you just weren't where they assumed you'd be.

It Won't Feel This Way Forever

That hurt. I know that hurt.
It's okay to let it hurt.
You don't have to pretend it doesn't.
But I also know that *you* know that it won't feel this way forever.

It won't feel this way forever.

And not because you numb it out or ignore it.
It won't feel this way forever because you're being with it right now.
Feel it hurt right now.
And it won't feel like this one day.

I know it feels hard to imagine that it wouldn't feel like this.

But I know you know that's true.
And I don't know when that will happen.
But I know it will, and you know it will.

I'm not saying it's not going to be there.
This will always be a piece of you.
But it's not always going to feel like this.
It's not always going to feel like this.

Be here with it.
Be here with me.

It won't feel this way forever.

I Loved You Then

We weren't talking about anything really.
Then suddenly you just said it.
"I loved you then, you know. I loved you so much.
It's overwhelming how much I loved you."
I didn't even realize what was happening.
"I loved you so much," you repeated, shaking your head slowly, tears falling.
I thought I was going to fall over, crash with the wave of it all.
"I loved you then," you said again.

THINGS I NEEDED TO SEE

I Knew You Were Real

Something was feeling off all day. I was agitated.

"What's going on?" I heard.

"Nothing, I don't know," I said.

"You can talk to me." Always such a gentle voice.

"You can talk to me, I'm right here."

I could feel myself fighting it. *I don't know, I don't know.*

You do know.

And I did.

Suddenly I'm sitting on the kitchen floor, crying, pushing my back against the cabinets.

"I wish you were here," I finally said.

"I am here, I'm right here. You are too."

But I didn't see.

"I wish you were here," I said again.

"Right here," you said softly.

Then I saw you.

Thanks to the one person who saw me.

Who I now believe. After all this time. Even though I wish it weren't true. I wasn't solid; they knew, before everything. And they helped me see it with three words, and not "I love you." Three words that only they and I will ever know mean anything special.

"I knew you were real," I finally said—to them, I thought.

But they fade away.

It wasn't them.

123456789101112

She's sitting on the ground. Knees pulled in, face down. Everything is dark.

"I know you."

She looks up. Her face is stone, but her body is shaking.

"I'm right here."

She feels a hand on her cheek. Soft and warm.

Her eyes close, and she shakes her head slowly, pulling away.

"I know you."

A hand on the back of her neck. Gentle.

Her body heaves, and the tears fall heavy. One hand on her cheek, one on the back of her neck, arms wrapped around her tightly. Tighter than ever.

She presses her face into the arms. Don't let go.

She opens her eyes and sees a hand outstretched.

"Reach for me."

She does. Once.

A small glow in her hand. The light on her face.

Exhale. It blossoms.

"When you're ready."

123456789101112

123456789101112

123456789101112

A fire is blazing. Sparking and crackling and jumping. Bright oranges and yellows. The sound is deafening, the room groaning as the fire swallows more and more of it. Watching. Everything is dark, but her outline is visible as she stares into the fire. The only thing moving is her thumb and middle finger, rubbing together.

The ash is flying; it falls all around her. Her eyes don't leave the fire. The smell is strong, and she takes a breath in. Deeper. All of it. Burning. This isn't hers. But all of it is hers. This is hers to burn.

Connecting

You're watching me work. I can feel you watching as I put things together down to the tiniest particle. I don't know what I'm expecting. Well, I do. All the pieces are there. I set it up so perfectly. Layered and intricate, and seamless. *Why isn't it connecting*? I keep trying. A million ways. A million times. *Try again. Keep trying, you'll get it.* I cringe. I know that tone. Urgent and tight. "Keep going no matter what" is more the meaning there.

You keep watching.

Why won't it connect? I don't understand. Everything is right, it should be connected. I check and recheck every point. *Yes, yes, that's going through, that's there.* But nothing. It doesn't make sense that it isn't connecting. It's worked before.

You smile slightly and raise an eyebrow.

My view gets smaller and smaller. Until there's just a sliver of light.

"Will you come on a walk with me?" you ask. "I don't know where we're going, but I know where to go."

And suddenly I hear two voices I recognize. But I've never met them. How could they know? They don't know me. Do they? One actually said my name. I furrow, looking over at my layered and intricate, and seamless, work. How hard I try. And still nothing there. But I feel it here.

“Yes, I’m lost,” one says with an acceptance in their eyes that I’ve never seen from anyone else. “It’s okay, it’s okay,” the other says so gently, holding out their hands. It’s like they’ve heard everything I’ve ever thought. Without trying.

Maybe in another time or world or universe we knew each other. I want to be rational about that last thought, but it’s honestly the only thing that makes sense.

The Backdrop

"Come back, please come back!" I hear her screaming.

But it drives away, the door closes, the back turns.

"Here, Love, I'm right here." I extend my hand to her, but she's facing away from me.

Pain doesn't care about age. Here it is.

The backdrop, the only thing she sees.

Characters may move around in front of it, time passes around it, but the backdrop is the same.

I finally see it there too.

I finally see what she sees.

She's still turned away from me.

"Please come back," she whispers.

My heart reaches for her.

Just be here with her.

Just love her.

I Remember You

The cloak is long but barely intact.
More like strands of fabric knotted together.
All tied on and through to stay as one.
It has to stay together.

I remember you.

The softest.
And then the hardest.
Remember this is you too.

The fabric strands flutter.
The sun is setting behind.
It reaches into the folds and unwraps what it protects.
What is has always protected.

Shrouded in layers and layers of it.
How long has it kept it safe?
Forever.
It doesn't want to let it go right away.
It feels like part of it, and it is.
But in time, it sees.

I remember you.

19

When the number 19 meant something.

19 years in.

19 years to walk back out.

The year 2019.

October 19.

And another 19 starting here.

There Is No Supposed To

I feel so wrong about so many things. Like I'm supposed to feel differently about them.

I thought I said it to myself, but you must have heard me because you said, "You're not wrong."

"Why do I feel wrong then?" I asked.

"I think because you think there's a right."

"There are wrongs and rights, though." I was sure of that.

You paused. "There are things that cause so much pain that I wish they never happened. I wish we didn't live in a world where terrible things happen. I wish people didn't take their pain out on other people, on any living thing. All humans do that in so many different ways. Sometimes they're not conscious of it, sometimes they do it intentionally. But how you feel about your things—that's not wrong. You don't have to feel a certain way about any of those things. There is no supposed to."

I could feel my eyes starting to roll. I kinda hated these conversations sometimes. "But I *am* supposed to," I said.

"You *think* you're supposed to. But you don't feel that way, right here, under everything—under fear, guilt, anger, everything peeled away. *That's* the truth, so there's this grating. You can try to bend and squeeze yourself into how you think it's supposed to be, you can disappear and think because you don't feel how it's supposed to feel that nothing matters...or you can take my hand and see that the supposed to doesn't actually exist."

We Can Never Be The Same

I know you showed me the trees are stone inside. That's okay. Trees are not the only things that root. And there's not just one way to do it. I can feel my roots winding around inside. They're strong but thin and wiry; they wrap around every inch, holding me in. They're in me, not going down. Where the thorns fell, that's where it starts. None of it was wasted, none of it was not needed, but it's different now. The thorn bushes were petrified, too, and I know we're under there. So much stone means so much time. Millions of years in a second.

Things may repeat but that does not mean they're the same. It isn't the same. Nothing is ever the same. We repeated actions before but that didn't make us the same; it made us more solid. Every time, every choice, more and more choices, deeper in. Until a different decision. Whatever happens, we are not the same. Sequences of events can happen similarly, but we are not the same. It looks familiar, but we are not the same. We can never be the same.

Every moment clears more or smudges more. But the amount of clear or smudge is not the same. Keep clearing or keep smudging. Of course, it will not stay a perfect amount of clear. Unlikely in this world. But if no clearing happens, the smudge just keeps getting thicker. For years. Until a different decision. Nothing about anything is the same.

Open To Fly

You have to be open to fly.

It's not hard.

It's soft.
It's soft.
It's soft.

The Edge Of The End

She's looking at the ground, and suddenly a yellow light appears below like it's under ice. It's all distorted but vibrant against the blue surface. The light glints off the gold specks in her eyes as they widen. The air is cold—this is where it all started.

The light gets stronger, pulsing against the ground. It starts gliding on the other side of the surface, moving away from her but beckoning her to follow. She rises so much easier this time and starts after it. She feels like she's flying and somehow knows she will be soon. The light pauses a couple times, checking if she's still following and then continuing on, lilting like her favorite song. It's dark all around—it's always dark here—but the light is bright and so is she.

She notices a point in the distance not too far off now. The light stops just ahead of her and presses itself against the other side of the ground until she feels the whole slab shift. It starts to slant; she digs her feet in, eventually putting a hand on the ground that's now right in front of her. She starts crawling up, scaling a cliff. The Edge is close. The ground she was standing on keeps shifting until she's climbing upside down. The light is hovering on the other side, without a face but full of expression. *You can do it*, it's saying, *Climb*. She knows she won't let go now.

She can see the world below her, everything she ever knew. All the fires still burning. One hand reaches the Edge, the Edge of the End. She feels her fingers crawl over it. The light intensifying. Her other hand makes its way, and she starts pulling herself up and over, her feet dangling in the End for just a second. One knee swings up and then the other, legs shimmering against the dark ground.

She takes a breath. It's still cold, but the kind of cold that feels like her whole body is open space, like the air can get into every single molecule. She stands up, and the light meets her eyes. She looks around, but nothing is there. She looks at the light again, questioning, the furrow in her brow as pronounced as ever. "Is there supposed to be something here?" she asks aloud. The light gestures out and then back to her, glowing. She takes a breath in. "Okay."

She Believed Me

Her eyes are lowered.
Her hair looks like it's been ripped out in fistfuls.
Maybe it has.

She's brutal.
In every way.
How she looks, how she feels, how her eyes stare down.

I've never seen anything like her.
But I know everything about her.
Sharp and harsh.

But she is other things too.
"I'm so sorry, sweet girl."
She stands still.

She hasn't been here in a long time.

I don't know where she was, but she came back.

She believed me and came back.

I'll Always Need You

"You don't need me anymore," you said to me.

"Yes, I do," I said quickly, firmly.

"Not the same way," you said, shaking your head.

"Maybe not the same way, but I'll always need you."

"Promise?" you asked, looking up.

A Petrified Forest

I've had visuals of it climbing up from the cave
and looking through a hole in a tree.
It can see both of us when it looks out and can
see us both looking back at it.
This time, the view expands out and it's a
petrified forest.
All the wood has turned to stone.

All the trees look the same, but she knew which
tree it was in.
She went and sat down at the trunk.
That's when I sat down there too, and started
pressing against it.
In the tree, it could feel me pressing against it.

And I looked at her sitting next to me.

She was trying to help, and she's all glowing and really determined.
The last piece of the image before I opened my eyes was her running her finger across one of her gold seams to get some gold on her finger.
And then she drew a gold line around and spiraling up the tree.

It was such a kind gesture.
Maybe just to let it know we're here.

I Hope She's Not Alone

Are you okay, hon?
Yeah, I'm just walking home.
Do you want a ride? It's raining, it's cold.
No, I'm almost there, but thanks.

She's scared.
I know that face.
I know that walk.
The rain and cold.

I hope someone's waiting.
I hope she's not alone.

Come With Us

Back in the square, but it was deserted.
Not quite light or dark.
What are we doing back here, I thought.
I looked at the statue in the middle.
Even I never really noticed it or looked at it there
in the middle of the square.
But it was comforting that it was always there.

Comforting that it was always there.

I cringed in that moment.
I looked at it.
Really looked at it for the first time.

And then everything got tingly.
A golden glow started emanating from the stone.

I couldn't believe I'd never thought to look at it
before.
It was so obvious but inside out.
I almost laughed thinking about the first time I
saw that statue.
How it had been there the whole time.

"Come with us," I said.
And I saw it soften, stone turning to warm light.
"Come with us," I said again.
I think it will.

Hurts To Remember

I could see it too clearly.
I wanted to forget it.

I tried everything to forget it.
Everything.

I thought I was afraid to remember.
Until they showed me.

Sometimes when it hurts to remember.
You're afraid to forget.

Dancing In The Field

She was dancing in the field.
Fireflies all around her.
They were all different colors—purple, blue, orange, and green.
She was twirling around and stomping her feet in the mossy wet ground.
The last of the sun and the start of the moon shining in the sea behind her.
She kept looking over at me, beckoning me to come dance with her.
She was laughing and smiling.
I wanted to but couldn't.
She didn't run over and grab me or pull me.
She just kept looking over, inviting.
Reaching out her hand, offering it to me.
I couldn't take it.

She wasn't frustrated though; she just kept smiling.

Knowing.

I could feel she knew.

Beginnings And Endings

It seems like it's easy to tell when things begin and end.

But it isn't easy here.

Beginnings come from unexpected places.

Not from nowhere, but not from where it seems they'd come maybe.

Stopping the search for beginnings, that's a task.

Wait for something to begin, and it never will.

And the moments that come with the hope of forever always end too soon.

In a way.

Not waiting and not hanging on forever.

That's where it begins.

And ends.

This Will Take A Bit

A cold basement.
She's shivering, needs more layers on.
I hand her a sweatshirt and sweatpants to wear
over what she has on.
Why hasn't anyone come to find her?
Why didn't I find her until now?
I feel sick when I think about it.
I feel guilty too.
And sad.
About so much.
This will take a bit to get through.

She won't even look at me.
And she's still shaking even with the layers on.
I'm glad she put them on at least.
That's something.

The floor is hard, frayed carpet.

I sit down next to her.

We have to get out of here, but I don't know how yet.

Not That Anymore

Nothing is falling apart or disappearing.

It's all changing into something else.

But I don't want to leave you like that.

"I'm not that anymore," you say. "You're
imagining me that way."

You walk over to me.

I never looked you in the eye, but this time I did.

"There. See? That's me," you say, shining.

You Always Saw Her

The curtain shifted. Something was behind it. *Don't rush*, I said to myself. Whatever is there will come out when it's ready.

But she went closer and slowly pulled the curtain aside. Then she screamed your name. The first time I saw her truly smile. The first time I saw her light up.

You came out from behind the curtain. Such a sweet face. And she hugged you. Her eyes squeezed close, burying her face in you; her arms holding you probably too tightly.

You were steady and calm like you always were. I wasn't expecting to see you again. I reached out, and you came over to me. Like you always did. Your eyes seeing right through me.

You always saw her. You were there for her when I wasn't. And you came back to be with her now.

The Sun Rises

And the sun rises.

And I know you.

She Knew The Way

The door was ajar.
We crept up to it slowly, quietly.
I could hear the music coming out.
Echoing through the giant space.

There were tall windows on the other side of the room, the length of the whole wall.
Thick curtains draping from them and sweeping the floor.
A chandelier in the center was partially lit.
A few slivers of light coming in through the curtained windows.
Otherwise the room was dark.

You didn't see us there.
I looked at her first.

She knew the way.

I had never seen this room before.

But she knew you were in there.

Big Hugs

I asked someone for a hug last night.
I've never done that.

He had on a gray sweater with little white flecks.

He didn't hesitate.
He's a big hugs kind of person.

Keeper Of The Roots

I don't know how I ended up on the floor in that room, but I did.
Leaning against the wall behind me and the cabinet to my side.
It felt like a good place to curl in maybe.
The room is dark when my eyes are open, but lights up when I close them.
And then I see her.
I haven't seen her in awhile, but she's always around.
Then suddenly red lavender is appearing from everywhere.
Remember when we first saw that?
Everything spiky and sharp turning to red blossoms.

She's spinning, looking at it all around her. And then a swirl of light, and she transforms from spiky and thorny to red lavender blossoms too, covering her head and fingers. Her eyes turn green. Everything that was thorns transforming, melting into red lavender. She touches a petal and then looks at me, as surprised as I am.

I'm so happy for her I feel like I'm going to burst. She puts her palm on the ground—dry, sandy soil. I feel her feeling the roots running through her too.

She is the root.
And she is the keeper of the roots.
She always has been.

THINGS I NEEDED TO UNDERSTAND

Where I Want To Meet You

Everything we do lives long after we die.
The worst, the best, and all in between.

Sometimes, some day, we realize all of it matters.
And none of it does.

But all the things we do don't end when we die.
Ask your deep pain, or your deep love.

So make your choice.
Knowing it all matters and doesn't.

And when all of this has fallen away.
That's where I want to meet you.

Never Disappeared

I've been thinking a lot about you.
How you're the only person who didn't disappear.
You're gone, but you never disappeared.
And I don't get that.
I've been trying to understand it, and I don't.

It's like you knew.
It's like you knew how not to disappear.

When I try to explain it to people, I don't have words for it.
I don't know this alphabet.
I don't know the letters even.
I don't understand how you could do that.

And sometimes I think, I'm giving you a lot of
credit.
For doing something that I thought I couldn't do.
Maybe it's that.
But, I think in this case, it's not that I'm giving
you too much credit.
Because that's what really happened.
That actually wasn't me imagining something.
You actually didn't disappear.
And I still don't know how.
How that works.

I can feel I'm trying so hard to understand it.
And trying to think of maybe what you would say
to me.
But I don't even know, I don't have a vocabulary
for it.
For what that is.

I wish you weren't gone.
But I'm also so glad you didn't disappear.
And maybe you wouldn't say anything to me in that.
Just let me get there when I get there.
Maybe now I'm giving you too much credit.

But that happened before anything else.
So, I guess what I'm saying is, I draw on that a lot.
On a few moments of you not disappearing.
And I don't have language for it, for how it feels.
Except you proved to me that it can exist.

One Beautiful Infinite Moment Of You

You were already open. You already knew. In one beautiful moment.

Remember you already knew, and it was so easy.

Before any of this, before anything, you knew.

You've worked really hard, and I'm glad that you have—you've stayed with it all.

And what incredible understanding has come from it.

But here we are at the beginning.

Remember you already knew.

You didn't actually have to do anything.

And also you did, because you had to understand it was already there.

A long path full of caves and oceans and forests, and we open our eyes back where it began.

You were already open. You already knew. One beautiful infinite moment of you.

A Little Extra Time

It's exactly a year since this all started.

Well, it started on February 29.

It's crazy it was a leap year that year.

I guess somewhere I knew that I needed a day like that to make a change.

It wasn't just going to happen on any day.

It needed a day, in a year, where it felt like there was a little extra time.

Epic In That Moment

Somewhere in you knew then. You didn't even know what would or could happen but you knew this: You knew it had to be body, mind, and heart. All need to believe. Each gets there when it gets there with every new thing.

You must have had the tiniest belief that it could be real. I smile when I think about you writing that then, how you brought that belief into existence here. You were epic in that moment.

And you remembered the message there deeply and reminded yourself somehow every day. In the light and space, and in the darkness of the cave. You listened—"You're going too fast, wait for me." You waited. You stayed.

What you did here, with no timeline or expectation, everyday things. So many. So many moments when you were exactly what you needed. Body, mind, heart. When you held yourself more tightly than anyone else could. When you leaned against the chair with the speaker pressed against you to feel the vibration. Deeper breaths than you have ever taken. Love, joy. What you wrote happened. Difficult, dark, scary, and hopeless moments also happened. But you stayed, every day.

Time, space, patience. Remember that with anything. Build up the belief for your body, mind, and heart. They're so powerful together. Your mind connects the pieces. Your body knows how far to go. Your heart feels when it's correct.

And remember, *we* aren't going anywhere, and we can go *anywhere*.

November

The Things I Don't Want To Hear

I spend a lot of time dreaming about beautiful things. About how something would feel if it went exactly how I wanted it to go. A form of overcorrection from always thinking bad things would happen—you know, a practice. And definitely I needed to overcorrect, and it has led to amazing things.

But today, I wanted to hear the terrible things. I wanted people to tell me the things I did not want to hear. *Call us to discuss these results. Back with their ex. Catastrophic. They never did. They're not coming home. They didn't make it. It will cost more to fix than it's worth.* All of those things were more what I wanted to hear today, and not because it's a cold, gray day.

“Tell me the truth,” I said to no one in particular. Because even though it felt terrible, the truth was actually more comforting. I say, “I don’t want to deal with it,” a lot. For so many things. Big things, small things. *I don’t want to deal with it.* Someone I know always says, “It’s fine, I don’t want it to be a fight.” And I ask them—why does it have to be a fight? So, okay, I’ve had to ask myself, why does it have to be dealt with, why does that insinuate there’s already a problem? Because even though I can imagine beautiful things, my instinct is, *This will be a problem.* So if all those things are true—the things I don’t really want to hear but also do—what would I have to deal with?

And the answer is just...me.

Just like it's me if all those things are not true. So am I really saying—about almost everything—I don't want to deal with me. I don't want to deal with me in this. Well, I think so. And what am I holding in order to not have to deal with me? What if everything fell away, nothing to deal with. What would be easier? And why does it have to be terrible to let it go? I think because then the decision is made for me. So all my beliefs about me can remain safe and intact.

The thing is, those beliefs aren't really me. I'm holding on to that stuff with fear and guilt glue. Extra strength. If I'm saying I want the truth, I have to be okay with it being the thing I don't want to hear. And also more than one thing can be true. But here, I can feel I'm waiting for the decision to be made for me. Something I don't like when it happens in other places.

So I get prepared, sit down, and look myself right in the eye. "Tell me the terrible thing," I say, and then, instinctively, I wonder how I'll deal with it.

Here's the truth about one of those things. The person said exactly the terrible thing in exactly the way I needed to hear it. How could they know? I never know how that works. But they told me the truth I needed to hear. *What do I wish someone would say?* is a practice I do all the time. It helps me understand where I am, what I'm seeking. And in some incredible moments, another person appears and says the exact thing I wished they'd say. I love it when that happens.

This is the opposite way. It hurts to hear the thing I really don't want to hear. But in this moment, I realized that it made me believe even more the things the person said that I needed to hear. I believe they told me the real thing both ways. And I realized I'd rather hear "the real" both ways than just the thing I want to hear. As beautiful as the thing I want to hear is, and I want to be in it forever, the truth of the thing I don't want to hear reinforces the truth of the thing I want to hear.

When I think about how they told me the terrible thing, I'm just amazed by them. They knew it would cause pain, but it was so clear that wasn't the intention. Pain is part of humans living human lives. And it wasn't their pain spilling out on me. In other ways, yes it was, but not in this moment. It took me a long time to understand it was the best delivery of a thing I never wanted to hear that I've ever experienced.

So, "Tell me the terrible thing," I say to myself again. *I've got you.* That's one of those beautiful things I needed to hear that someone said to me. And here, I'm saying it to myself over and over. I believed them, can I believe me?

"Be truthful about the things you don't want to hear," I say to myself. "Be truthful just like you are with the things you do want to hear. I've got you. Pain isn't the intention. I've got you."

Because Of You

Don't give away your power to them.

It wasn't them, it was you.

It wasn't their belief, it was yours.

It wasn't their love, it was yours.

It isn't because of them, it's because of you.

Ruthless

I've been listening to this song for five days now,
and I can't get enough.
I love it every time it starts again.
I feel it in my body.
I feel myself seeing me.
I feel the ruthlessness churn.
I feel it feeling understood.

At that one part, it sways.
This is its song.
It knew it when it heard it.
It led me to it.
It was ready to be understood.

How it has always been there.
How it knew me.

How it is me.

But I didn't know me.
Not like this.

I know the feeling.
Deep.
Relentless.
It finds a way.

I can't say how it did then.
Or then.
Or so many times.
But it did.

Covered over, buried, hidden, but it's been there.
And I can see how it was kept safe.

You kept it safe.

From everything.

Somehow you did.

You wrapped it up and folded it in.

You shrouded it, but it was still me.

It was always me.

You protected me in every way, and even you were no match for it.

Fear keeps searching.

But I'm ruthless.

I'm ruthless while the fear is scampering and swirling for moments, days, years.

Ruthless is so patient and unwavering.

So maybe that story about me is true, but not in the way I thought.

One Thing Instead Of Another

I used to wish you'd choose me, you know.
Choose me over your guilt, over your fear.
But I see now that we're all just choosing how to survive in each moment.
Every moment is a choice.
It doesn't feel like it always, and I wasn't aware of it always, but it is.
I used to think I was choosing you.
That I cared more about you than me.
But that's not exactly accurate.
I wanted you to care.
I wanted you to pick me.
And I tried to get you to see that.
But that was because that's what I thought I needed.
Not what you needed.

And I'm not you.

Every moment of our lives has been different.

I understand now why you couldn't and still don't choose me.

Because you had to choose you.

And choosing you meant choosing that.

I'm sure it didn't feel like a choice, but it was.

And I made mine.

How can I get through this moment?

What do I need to do or say or act on to get through this moment?

We're always choosing one thing instead of another.

We're always choosing what we think we need to survive.

Imagination

You're skeptical.
That's okay.

So I'll just write this.

Sometimes imagination isn't to escape, it's to understand.

Finish Making The Cake

Remember how you used to try to mix cake
batter the other way to get the eggs back?
Three stirs to the right, three stirs to the left,
and you hoped the eggs would reappear intact.

But once the eggs are in, they're part of it. No
undoing them.
Whether you're the one who cracked them open
or not.

You can stir to the left forever, but the eggs are
not going to come out.

Let's finish making the cake instead.
The eggs are just part of it; they're not all of it.

So instead of only seeing the eggs as separate
and focusing that they won't come out—

What if you saw the cake that can come from all
of this.
It can be whatever kind of cake you want, and
you can add whatever you want to it.

But let's try pausing the frantic mixing to the left.
Imagine if you finished making the cake instead.

Today It Wasn't Hard

Asking for help is really hard.
I think there are a lot of experiences that can undermine it, too.
That time I sought help and was dismissed.
Like I shouldn't need help.
Sometimes there was just no one to ask.
Sometimes trust was the factor.
I didn't believe the other person could help.
Sometimes it felt like they didn't understand the kind of help I needed.

All of that still exists and can still make asking for help hard, I think.

But today it wasn't hard.

All of a sudden.

Just once I got the answer I always needed.
A lot led up to it, but the asking-for-help itself
wasn't difficult.
What was I expecting?
I thought it would be hard because it always
seemed hard before.

But today it wasn't.

My Story Of You

Well, that was a big screaming mess. I didn't think it would be with you. I didn't even see it coming, then suddenly it was pouring out of me. Not something either of us expected, everything tearing apart. Actually, I won't say either of us—I don't know what you expected. I didn't even see your reaction.

I screamed a horrible thing. I wasn't calm. It wasn't beautiful. It was gross and raging. To be honest, it felt slimy. Slimy as I screamed at you what I was always scared you would scream at me. But you didn't scream at me that day. You said: "You've been fighting for me forever. At least now you're fighting for you."

So many different kinds of love. And some don't last forever. I think we all know that in a way. That doesn't mean it wasn't real, though; there are just different loves. And maybe forever doesn't mean what we think. Because I also remember one second. One second when you loved me. And it's a forever. So, some love, some love goes beyond this world, beyond that moon, beyond those stars. Bring the red and blue and meet me in the purple.

I wanted you to be something. But you aren't that. Because you're exactly you. I made you something else—wanted you to be someone you aren't. The thing I hate when people do to me. And I did it to you. Because of course I did. That's why I hate it when people do it to me. I thought maybe I was imagining the best of you. That can be a beautiful thing. But here, it was just what I wanted you to be. Not who you are. I so wanted it to be a certain way. I tried to make you for me. But like so much with so many, it wasn't actually about you. Another thing I hate when people do to me.

It's sad to watch it crumble, though. Watching it all fall apart. My story of You. I guess I always knew it was this way. Nothing you did to create it or undo it really. You were always you. I wanted you to be something I could hang on to. No deal made with you there, I just decided. I'm sorry. It took me a long time to understand that I didn't have to destroy your story of Me. I had to destroy my story of You.

Insist On It

I won't see you anymore?
No, not like this.
This is the only way I know.
That doesn't mean it's the only way there is.
But it won't be like this?
No, it won't be like this.
I don't want it to change.
I know. Remember when you didn't think
anything could change?
This is different.
It isn't. We forever begin. Insist on it.

The Human Who Created It

I first saw the picture two years ago. More than the writing on the webpage, it was the little illustration that caught my attention. It seemed so much gentler than the words. I found myself thinking about that picture often. So I started looking for where it came from. A beautiful book with a message I had not seen before. It made so much sense. This is the book I wish I had when I was a kid. But I have it now.

And when I wrote to the author, she responded. I asked if that image from that day two years ago was available as a print. She said she could make it one. And she mailed it to me from across the sea, packaged so carefully. I was amazed at the time she must have spent to ensure its safety.

She clearly cared about it, too. And now I have that beautiful print, from that page, two years ago. Not by copying it from a website. But from the human who created it. Who printed it on thick, canvas-like paper, who signed and dated it, who wrote a note saying this was a "lovely reminder" for her to "keep writing stories."

I feel really disconnected from people a lot of the time. I expect it actually. I decided it was easier than feeling the universe-imploding moments. But, it turns out, we humans can create universe-connecting moments for each other, too. In an instant. And unexpectedly, it seems. No wonder such moments surprise me.

So I let myself wander where universes inexplicably connected. And so much appears—A photo of me lit up like a trillion stars in the arms of the first person I boundlessly loved. The sunrise soul who said, "Stand close, if you want to," right as I was fading into an endless night. A smile from the one who is not afraid to see and hold all of me. The song that changed everything, and the kindness of the artist when I told him.

The disconnect is a real feeling, I still feel it often. And yet. I also have proof, on the table next to me and in all the exactly-what-I-needed moments, that not everything is disconnected all the time. A lovely reminder.

That One Costume

I remember the first time I felt emotions through a song.
How I repeated the tape and then the CD until they broke.
I couldn't get enough of how real it felt, even through crackly speakers.

And even though I knew they were actors, they seemed to be really feeling it.
They were humans.

I didn't understand how they could emote like that.
How their voices rose and fell, the urgency or gentleness, the sadness or anger.

I didn't understand it, but I couldn't stop listening.

I heard the song again today, with the fuller orchestration, and it brought me right back.
That one costume was so specific.
And not one that people thought made sense for an elementary school kid.

I remember no one knew who I was supposed to be, but I didn't care.

And when I listen to this now, it's so clear.

More Than Skin And Bones

People always seem to be fascinated with how strong a baby's grip is. How something so tiny can be so strong. It makes sense, though, doesn't it? Feeling lovingly held or feeling someone or something safe we can hold—emotionally, physically. There's something powerful in that, something more than skin and bones. Of course babies have a strong grip.

So at what point do we start telling ourselves to "let go" of things? I know what the intention is there, but it seems to be applied pretty universally, and, like all things, every experience is different for everyone. I believe some things do need to be gripped and held. Not everything maybe, but it's funny how holding on to something can have such a negative connotation. Like everything should be let go at some point. Maybe it's just semantics, but I don't believe everything needs to be let go.

So before I tell myself to "let go," I see what maybe needs to feel that hold—either me holding it or it holding me. What's scared or hurt or angry. Sometimes that needs holding, even gripping, not letting go. At least until it believes it doesn't need a hold.

But some of what I grip is intense, fiercely held. It actually needs to believe I won't let go...ever.

I know what feels correct for me—to hold; to let go; to hold and then let go; to not even let go, maybe something just melts; to never let go...and I'm the only one who knows for me.

The Sea

I think you want to come back.

I think you do.

Will you come with me?

We can find the sea.

I know we can if we both want it.

Stay right here with me.

We can do this.

All My Favorites

I'm watching the movie for probably the two thousandth time.

I'm not sure if it's my favorite movie, but it has my favorite scene with my favorite character saying my favorite lines all accompanied by my favorite part of a score.

It took two thousand times, but today, I finally understand why they're all my favorites.

And then, as though you've always known,

"I love you that much," you say, pausing as you walk through the room, right as all my favorites are rising together.

And then, as I realize I've always known,

I love you that much too.

I Love How

I love how you know exactly what you need.
I love how you shook off everything I put on and over and around you and then looked at me.
Extra fluffy from the shake.

I love how when someone said, "You don't look pretty, if that's what you're going for."
You said, "Good," and walked away. I laugh when I think about it.
That isn't what you were going for.

I love how you know when something is right for you.
A song, a someone, a choice.
Even if no one else understands.

I love how you are.

Extra fluffy now. Nothing on or over or around.

I won't get in your way—go be what I love.

A STORY

The Turn

I turn around, and you're there. I wasn't expecting to see you. "Hi," I gasp, and then I crumble. My ribs separating with each breath, my eyes stinging with tears. You slowly touch my arm and then pause. I lean into you and you hug me tightly. I feel you squeeze the top of my left shoulder. I don't know why that makes me cry more, but it does. The bringing back, maybe. My head is pulsing, and I push my forehead into your arm. You put your hand on the back of my neck. And we just stand there.

The Stay

The app thought I was in Inverness, then in Rome weirdly, but I wasn't. I hadn't even checked in. My battery was running out. You walked with me the whole time. You sat there with me. I said, "Don't you have to go?" You did, your flight was in an hour. But you stayed. I don't even remember being angry or frustrated about how the itinerary was messed up; it just felt so good that you were with me. You held the phone. You found a place to charge. You weren't rushing or pushing. Feels like time, space, and patience to me. Maybe you would call it something else. But I can feel myself trying to gather it all up, trying to hold on to it. I can never hold enough of it though.

The Conversation

I had all kinds of things I wanted to say. How much I wanted to thank you, I thought. So I started speaking and then paused.

"I don't want to wait for you."

That wasn't the plan, but it just came out—not that I *couldn't* even wait, I just didn't want to. I was shocked at myself.

"I never wanted you to wait for me," you said quietly.

"But what will you do?" I asked, my voice breaking as the tears started.

"Please don't assume I need you."

Your voice was gentle, but the words felt harsh.

I bristled but then thought, fair enough.

You never said you wanted me to wait or asked me to wait.

"I'm afraid you won't feel loved," I whispered.

"Is that me or you?" you replied.

Also harsh, I thought, but not unfair or untrue even.

I had to take a few breaths.

"Yeah, I guess that's me."

You never took your eyes off me, always so steady there.
I've never been able to do that like you can.
"Please don't wait for me," you said.

And in that moment, I want you to say, *But we'll meet up again sometime*, but you don't. And I know it isn't true so I'm glad you don't say it, even though I want you to. I admire that about you.

"Go on," you said. "This isn't leaving behind, it's just leaving to go your own way."
But it feels the same to me—and not leaving is everything. Or I thought it was.
"Leave this door open, that's all. Go on."
But I'm frozen. I'm scared I won't hear your voice again.

"It's not leaving like you think it is," you said, reading my mind. "Remember things may not be what you think they are."

The Share

I talked to someone else about this today.
That was different.
I asked them how they felt about patience.
They laughed. "Oh, I don't have any," they said quickly.
We talked about that.
I said my experience of them was they were always very open with time.
They laughed again. "Yeah, I'm a good listener I guess."
"Yeah, you definitely are," I said, "but maybe that isn't what you think of as patience."

I'm still reeling from when I said, *I don't want to wait for you*. I'm feeling like I'm actually impatient when I always thought I was patient. But I don't say that, even though I'm feeling it all swirl inside me.

And then they said, "If you want to share more of what's going on, you can, but no pressure."
Like they saw it.
So I did share a bit more—not all of it, but a bit more.
It didn't feel scary to talk to them. They are open with time, and there was space, and to me there was patience. I don't even think they were aware they offered me all of that. And they offered it so easily and without hesitation. Feels a bit scary how easy it was.

The Realization

A lot of things have been different. That one actor who I was so scared of in one place was actually the sweetest in another place. I know that's their job, but it weirded me out a bit because they were completely, and convincingly, the opposite. From the scariest to the gentlest. I still don't really understand how that can be shifted so extremely. But what I thought is also shifting. Even though I think I'm scared of it, maybe it isn't scary. But this is old, deep. Maybe the deepest.

I tie it all together—all the patience, all the leaving, all the not leaving, all the "being there." *Is that me or you?*—I keep hearing those words in my head. Someone seeing me exactly accurately, cutting right through miles of debris that I've been digging around in for years with my fingers. Cutting right through whatever character—scary, sweet. They knew it was neither and both and all the rest. The worst thing, the cruelest thing, maybe isn't what I think it is. This is the only time, so far, I've felt that. It's an incredible feeling—hopelessly sad and the most beautiful. Their understanding me like that is also hopelessly sad and the most beautiful. I can feel I'm trying to hold on to it again, but again, I can never hold enough of it. *It's okay, go on*, you said.

Thank you to so many.

I needed all of you.

And to the one at the end—thank you for loving me through the absolute deepest water, all the way to the core.

Taylor ended up where she least expected to end up, so it's where it all had to happen. She has a podcast called "Eyes Closed Practice" in which she reads entries and shares music from those practices. Under an artist name, she has also released several singles and two albums. One album is spoken word and the other is a musical that will (one day) be on a stage.

Printed in the USA
CPSIA information can be obtained
at www.ICGtesting.com
CBHW021633300724
12432CB00013B/288